This
book is
DELISH!

NATIONAL GEOGRAPHIC
KiDS

BRAiN CANDY 3

SUPER JUICY!

Seriously Sweet Facts
to Satisfy Your Curiosity

NATIONAL GEOGRAPHIC
WASHINGTON, D.C.

HAVE YOU EVER WONDERED ...

Fact-alicious!

...JUST HOW COLD IT IS IN SPACE?

...HOW LOUD A LION'S ROAR IS?

...WHAT LIFE WAS LIKE ABOARD A PIRATE SHIP?

WELCOME TO *BRAIN CANDY 3,* A SCRUMPTIOUS SET OF JUICY TIDBITS, TELLING TRUTHS, UNCANNY CONNECTIONS, AND MIND-BLOWING FACTS.

Each spread in *Brain Candy 3* starts with a fact nugget and then gives you more to nibble on with related revelations. For example, elephants have thick skin, but just how thick is the surface of this massive mammal? It's 50 times thicker than yours and can weigh as much as 2,000 pounds (900 kg)! Earth's smaller animals offer some sweet surprises, too. Hop on a honeybee to discover how hardworking these fast-flying insects are. They beat their wings 200 times a second as they fly to two million flowers to make just one pound (.45 kg) of honey. And speaking of phenomenal figures, Jupiter is the biggest planet in our solar system, but just how big is the fifth planet from the sun? More than 1,300 Earths would fit inside it.

LIKE LEARNING COOL FACTS AND HOW THEY'RE CONNECTED? TREAT YOUR BRAIN TO A SWEET FACT RUSH WITH *BRAIN CANDY 3.*

JUPITER IS MASSIVE.

More than
1,300
Earths
would fit inside
the planet.

WHOA!
I thought
my backyard
was big.

6

If you walked **10 miles** (16 km) a day, it would take **74.8 years** to walk around **Jupiter's equator.**

Jupiter's **Great Red Spot,** the solar system's longest-lasting storm, is about **10,000 miles** (16,100 km) **wide.**

7

PIZZA IS MADE FOR PERSONALIZING.

Bone
APPÉTIT!

Legend holds that **Margherita pizza** was first made in **1889** in Naples for Queen Margherita—its white, red, and green ingredients **represent the Italian flag.**

A U.S. pizza franchise makes a **grilled cheese** crust.

One pizzamaker in New York City offered a pizza with a **whole lobster—** head included—as a topping.

A Boston, U.S.A., **doughnut-maker** sold **pepperoni pizza doughnuts.**

SOME LAND ANIMALS ARE SURPRISINGLY GOOD

SWIMMERS.

SLOTHS SWIM **THREE TIMES FASTER** THAN THEY MOVE ON LAND.

PIGS SWIM IN OCEAN WATERS OFF AN ISLAND IN THE BAHAMAS.

MOOSE CAN **DIVE UP TO 20 FEET** (6 M) TO FEED ON PLANTS AT THE BOTTOM OF LAKES.

ELEPHANTS ARE CAPABLE OF **SWIMMING UP TO 30 MILES** (48 KM) AT ONE TIME, USING THEIR TRUNK AS A SNORKEL.

JUST AS
EACH PERSON
HAS A
UNIQUE
SET OF
FINGERPRINTS...

I'm no COPYCAT!

NO TWO **TIGERS** HAVE THE SAME **STRIPE PATTERN.**

WHALE SHARKS EACH HAVE A DISTINCT **SPOT PATTERN.**

LIONS' WHISKER HOLES FORM **UNIQUE PATTERNS.**

KOALAS HAVE THEIR OWN **UNIQUE FINGERPRINTS,** TOO—AND THEY LOOK JUST LIKE A HUMAN'S!

SOME **FLOWERS** CAN

FOOL YOU...

THE RARE **MONKEY ORCHID** LOOKS LIKE A **MONKEY'S FACE.**

Wow! Just like lookin' in the MIRROR!

THE **"DARTH VADER" PLANT** GETS ITS NICKNAME FROM ITS FLOWER, WHICH RESEMBLES **VADER'S MASK.**

THE **WHITE EGRET ORCHID** LOOKS LIKE AN **EGRET IN FLIGHT.**

Here I COME!

...and others can DISGUST you.

16

THE **CORPSE FLOWER** SMELLS LIKE **ROTTING FLESH.**

THE **AFRICAN STARFISH FLOWER'S** TERRIBLE SMELL **ATTRACTS FLIES,** WHICH HELP POLLINATE THE PLANT.

SKUNK CABBAGE, A FLOWERING PLANT, EMITS A **SKUNKLIKE ODOR.**

MILLIONS OF SHIPWRECKS ARE WAITING TO BE DISCOVERED.

I am PURR-fect for the job!

Of the estimated **three million** shipwrecks on the ocean floor, LESS THAN ONE PERCENT **have been explored.**

An estimated **U.S. $60 billion** of SUNKEN TREASURE remains **unrecovered.**

Bermuda has MORE SHIPWRECKS per square mile than anywhere else in the world.

Rusted bow of the R.M.S. Titanic

UNDERWATER TREASURE TROVES

Robert Ballard, the oceanographer who discovered the shipwreck of the R.M.S. *Titanic* in 1985, once said that more history lies underwater than in all the world's museums combined.

The 300-year-old shipwreck of the infamous pirate Blackbeard's *Queen Anne's Revenge,* which was found in 1996 off the North Carolina, U.S.A., coast, contained a bounty of artifacts. Onboard were 30 cannons—nine of which were still loaded—as well as navigational tools and gold.

More than 100 years ago, an ancient Roman shipwreck discovered off the coast of the Greek island of Antikythera included a shoebox-size bronze instrument. At first, historians were mystified, but later they determined that it was a complex mechanical "computer" that could track cycles of the solar system with exceptional accuracy.

One of the largest shipwreck treasures ever found was onboard a Spanish Navy ship that sank off the coast of Portugal in 1804. Seventeen tons (15 t) of silver coins worth hundreds of millions of dollars were discovered on it in 2007—which is certainly worthy of a "shiver me timbers"!

The Antikythera navigational tool from the fourth century B.C.

VENDING MACHINES
AREN'T JUST FOR CANDY.

IN JAPAN, SOME VENDING MACHINES ARE STOCKED WITH **NECKTIES.**

YOU CAN GET A **FRESH PIZZA** IN **THREE MINUTES** FROM A VENDING MACHINE IN ITALY.

YOU CAN **PICK OUT A CAR** FROM AN EIGHT-STORY VENDING MACHINE IN NORTH CAROLINA, U.S.A.

YOU CAN BUY A **LIVE CRAB** FROM A VENDING MACHINE IN CHINA.

KIDS CAN GET A **FREE BOOK** AT VENDING MACHINES IN NEW YORK CITY.

23

IF YOU LOOK CLOSELY, YOU CAN SPOT UNUSUAL GARGOYLES ON CHURCHES.

There is a **DARTH VADER CARVING** on the side of the **WASHINGTON NATIONAL CATHEDRAL** in Washington, D.C.

Comin' in for a **CLOSE-UP...**

GIZMO from the movie *Gremlins* appears as a gargoyle on a church in **NANTES, FRANCE.**

A gargoyle in the form of a **MAN PICKING HIS NOSE** is seen on a cathedral in **ENGLAND.**

ANTARCTICA IS BONE-CHILLING...

It holds the **RECORD** for the **COLDEST TEMPERATURE** on Earth—an estimated **MINUS 144°F** (-98°C).

BREATHING IN AIR THIS COLD for more than a few breaths would cause **HUMAN LUNGS TO FAIL**.

Feels **JUST RIGHT** to me!

Within five minutes at **MINUS 40°F** (-40°C) and **A MODERATE BREEZE,** human skin becomes **FROSTBITTEN**.

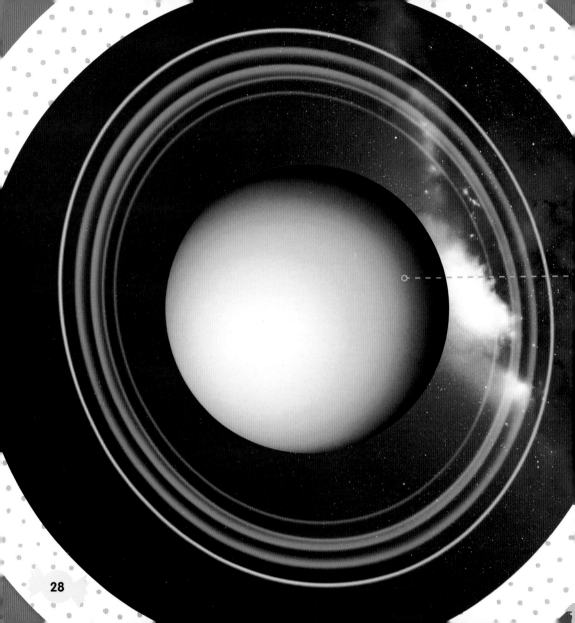

...BUT SPACE IS COLDER.

BRING IT.

THE COLDEST PLANET in our solar system is **URANUS—** its atmosphere dips down to **MINUS 371°F** (-224°C).

ASTRONAUTS' SPACE SUITS ARE BUILT to withstand temperatures of **MINUS 250°F** (-157°C).

AT MINUS 458°F (-272°C), **THE BOOMERANG NEBULA**, located in an area around **A DYING STAR**, is the **COLDEST KNOWN PLACE IN THE UNIVERSE.**

29

COTTON CANDY GOES BY MANY NAMES.

TRASH CAN BECOME TREASURE.

Kenyan artists use washed-up flip-flops found on local beaches to create **COLORFUL ARTWORK.**

Beads made from recycled paper have been used to create **MULTICOLORED BRACELETS** and **NECKLACES.**

Nobody will STEP on me now!

Some sportswear companies use recycled plastic in their **RUNNING SHOES.**

CHEETAH MOMS call for their cubs by making a **birdlike chirp.**

A **TIGER'S ROAR** is **louder than a gas lawn mower.**

COUGARS sometimes use a **loud scream** to communicate.

POOP CAN BE RECYCLED.

Look, Mom! I'm FAMOUS!

PANDA POO
盒装纸面巾

A Chinese company makes FACIAL TISSUES by blending PANDA POOP and BAMBOO LEAVES.

During the American Civil War, soldiers made **EXPLOSIVES** from **DRIED BAT POOP.**

A Thai elephant conservation center recycles **ELEPHANT POOP** into **PAPER**—each elephant makes enough for more than 100 pages a day!

100% 竹浆

400 张

PANDA POO

POOPAPER
MADE FROM POO

INSECTS CAN BE SUPER STRONG.

ALLEGHENY MOUND ANTS CAN LIFT **1,000 TIMES** THEIR BODY WEIGHT—THE EQUIVALENT OF A **175-POUND (80-KG) PERSON** LIFTING A FULLY LOADED **PASSENGER PLANE!**

A **HORNED DUNG BEETLE** CAN DRAG **1,141 TIMES** ITS WEIGHT— THAT'S LIKE A HUMAN PULLING **SIX DOUBLE-DECKER BUSES!**

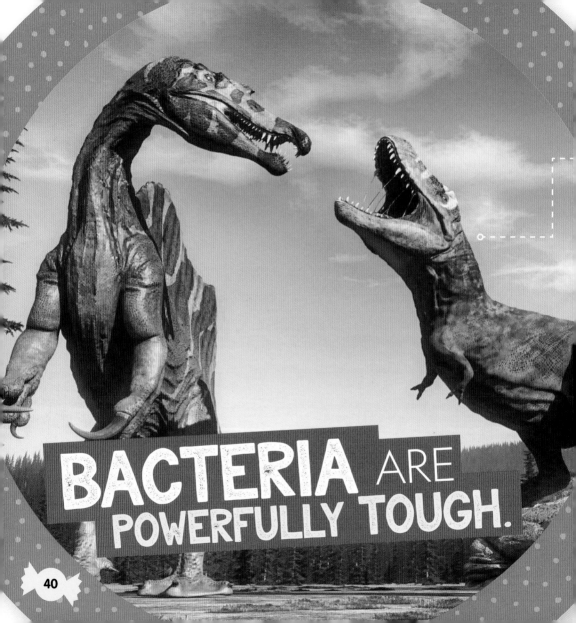

BACTERIA ARE POWERFULLY TOUGH.

They have **outlasted dinosaurs.**

There are more bacteria that live in **your gut's acidic environment** than there are **people on Earth.**

Some bacteria can **eat through rock.**

They live in the **severe weather** and **below-freezing** temperatures found on **Mount Everest.**

SPORTS EQUIPMENT CAN

SURPRISE YOU.

Time to
burn some
RUBBER!

IN **12TH-CENTURY** ITALY, MONKS PLAYED AN **EARLY VERSION OF TENNIS,** USING THEIR HANDS AS RACKETS.

A SOCCER BALL FROM THE **1540s** WAS **FOUND BEHIND A WALL** IN STIRLING CASTLE IN SCOTLAND—IT WAS MADE FROM A **PIG'S BLADDER.**

SOME **EARLY HOCKEY PUCKS** WERE MADE BY **GLUING TWO PIECES** OF A **RUBBER TIRE TOGETHER.**

THE **PLATYPUS** IS ONE UNUSUAL MAMMAL.

FOLDS OF SKIN cover its eyes and ears to keep water out.

The **DUCKLIKE WEBBING** on its front feet is **RETRACTABLE** for on-land gripping.

It finds food by detecting **ELECTRIC SIGNALS** with its bill.

It is one of only two mammals that **LAY EGGS.** (The other is the echidna.)

The male has **STINGERS** on its **HEELS** that deliver **VENOM.**

FRUITS CAN COME IN

STRANGE

SHAPES AND COLORS.

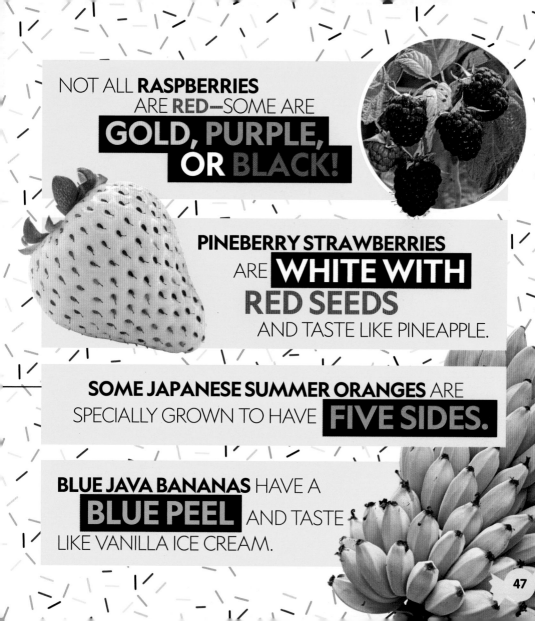

NOT ALL **RASPBERRIES** ARE **RED**—SOME ARE **GOLD, PURPLE, OR BLACK!**

PINEBERRY STRAWBERRIES ARE **WHITE WITH RED SEEDS** AND TASTE LIKE PINEAPPLE.

SOME JAPANESE SUMMER ORANGES ARE SPECIALLY GROWN TO HAVE **FIVE SIDES.**

BLUE JAVA BANANAS HAVE A **BLUE PEEL** AND TASTE LIKE VANILLA ICE CREAM.

SOMETIMES ANIMALS DANCE.

To share information about a food source with fellow workers, **HONEYBEES** perform the **WAGGLE DANCE**, wiggling back and forth in a straight line.

FERRETS perform a **HOP-AND-TWIST DANCE** when they've cornered prey, perhaps to confuse it.

Male **BLUE-FOOTED BOOBIES** do a **CLUMSY DANCE** to attract females.

Male **WILSON'S BIRDS-OF-PARADISE** show off their feathers and **HOP AROUND** in a dance to impress females perched nearby.

U.S. DOLLARS ARE NOTEWORTHY.

Did I make that MESS?

Bills are durable: You would have to fold a note **4,000 times** forward and backward to **tear** it.

When a **$100 bill** is moved back and forth, a **ribbon woven** into the bill causes images of bells and the number 100 to appear alternately.

Paper money isn't made of paper—it's **75 percent cotton** and **25 percent linen.**

VENOM CAN BE
DEADLY ...

Two drops of a **black mamba's venom can kill a person**—and its fangs can hold **20 drops.**

Don't **STEP** on me!

The venom of a **Sydney funnel-web spider** is capable of killing a person within **15 minutes.**

A **box jellyfish's lethal venom instantly stuns prey** so that an escape attempt won't damage the jellyfish's tentacles.

The **golf-ball-size blue-ringed octopus** packs enough venom to kill **26 humans.**

... BUT IT CAN ALSO SAVE LIVES.

ANTIVENOM— medicine that **OFFSETS THE EFFECTS OF A HARMFUL BITE OR STING—** is made from that creature's venom.

Venom from the world's most **VENOMOUS SNAKES** is used as a **BLOOD THINNER** for people at risk of blood clots.

GILA MONSTERS' VENOMOUS SALIVA has been made into a **DRUG FOR DIABETES** patients: It stimulates the human body's insulin production.

IF ALL OF EARTH'S HISTORY

WERE CONDENSED INTO

24 HOURS ...

12:10

AT **12:10 A.M.,** EARTH COLLIDES WITH ANOTHER PLANET, CREATING **THE MOON.**

4:00

AT **4:00 A.M.,** LIFE BEGINS WITH **ONE-CELLED ORGANISMS.**

9:52

AT **9:52 P.M.,** **MARINE ANIMALS** COME INTO EXISTENCE.

10:56

AT **10:56 P.M.,** **DINOSAURS** FIRST ROAM EARTH.

11:58

AT **11:58:43 P.M.,** **MODERN HUMANS** EVOLVE.

57

THE **OLYMPICS** HAVE **CHANGED** OVER TIME.

I've got the right MOVES!

IN **ANCIENT GREECE,** ATHLETES COMPETED **NAKED.**

IN THE FIRST MODERN OLYMPICS, IN **1896,** ATHLETES IN THE **ROPE CLIMB EVENT** WERE JUDGED NOT ONLY FOR THEIR SPEED BUT ALSO FOR THEIR STYLE OF CLIMB.

HOT-AIR BALLOONING WAS A DEMONSTRATION SPORT IN THE **1900** OLYMPICS.

A SPORT CALLED **SINGLESTICK** APPEARED ONLY IN THE **1904** OLYMPICS: COMPETITORS ATTEMPTED TO HIT EACH OTHER WITH BLUNT WOODEN STICKS!

An Olympic champion being crowned

THE OLYMPIC GAMES IN
ANCIENT GREECE

Athletic performances that awe a crowd are year-round events today—from gymnastics world championships to Super Bowls to World Cup soccer matches. But in ancient Greece, the main event was the Olympic Games, which began in 776 B.C. The Olympics were part of a religious festival honoring Zeus, the father of the Greek gods and goddesses. The event was held in Olympia, Greece, and athletes (all of whom were male), came from as far away as present-day Spain and Turkey to compete. While everyone from farmhands to the wealthy elite could enter, the majority of athletes were soldiers.

Records show that the first Olympics had just one event: a 600-foot (183-m)-long footrace. Later Olympic events included running, jumping, throwing, boxing, wrestling, and chariot racing.

There weren't any winter events in ancient Greece's Olympics—skiing and ice skating didn't appear until 1924, when the first modern winter Olympics were held in France. And instead of going for the gold, ancient Greek athletes hoped to win the coveted crown: a wreath woven from olive branches. Victors also received a hero's welcome—and perhaps even prize money—when they returned home.

Depiction of Olympic runners in ancient Greece

THE RING OF FIRE

IN THE PACIFIC OCEAN CAN

SHAKE, RATTLE, AND ROLL.

THE **25,000-MILE** (40,200-KM)-LONG **BELT** IS HOME TO MORE THAN **450 ACTIVE** VOLCANOES.

THE
9.5 MAGNITUDE
VALDIVIA EARTHQUAKE,
THE **LARGEST ON
RECORD,** HAPPENED
OFF THE COAST
OF CHILE
IN 1960.

IN SPRING 2015,
MAGMA ERUPTING
FROM SUBMARINE
VOLCANO **AXIAL
SEAMOUNT** OFF
THE COAST OF OREGON,
U.S.A., CAUSED MORE
THAN **37,000**
EXPLOSIONS.

SOME WATER CREATURES HAVE WACKY ADAPTATIONS.

TO **BREATHE UNDERWATER,** THE **WATER SCORPION** USES A **SNORKEL-LIKE TUBE** ON ITS BELLY.

THE **DIVING BELL SPIDER** SURVIVES UNDERWATER BY **BREATHING** FROM AN **AIR BUBBLE** IT TRAPS IN ITS WEB.

THE OCTOPUS IS OTHERWORLDLY.

Its **SKIN** can sense and respond to **LIGHT**, just like its **EYES CAN**.

Its **INK IS SO TOXIC** that if it didn't **SWIM AWAY** from its ink cloud, it could **DIE**.

It has **NINE BRAINS—ONE** of which is shaped like a **DOUGHNUT**.

The **OCTOPUS** has **THREE HEARTS**. One of the hearts **STOPS BEATING** when the octopus swims.

HOT DOGS

AREN'T ALWAYS SERVED ON BUNS AT U.S. MINOR LEAGUE BASEBALL PARKS.

Got any LEFT-OVERS?

IN SPRINGFIELD, ILLINOIS,
THE **JUMBO SPUD DOG
IS SERVED BETWEEN
TWO HALVES** OF A
BAKED POTATO.

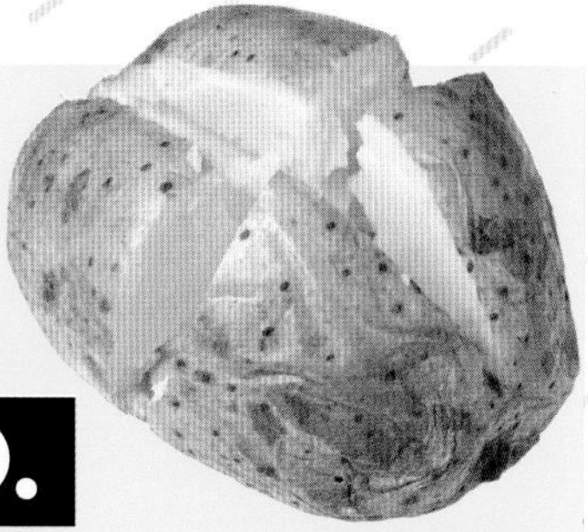

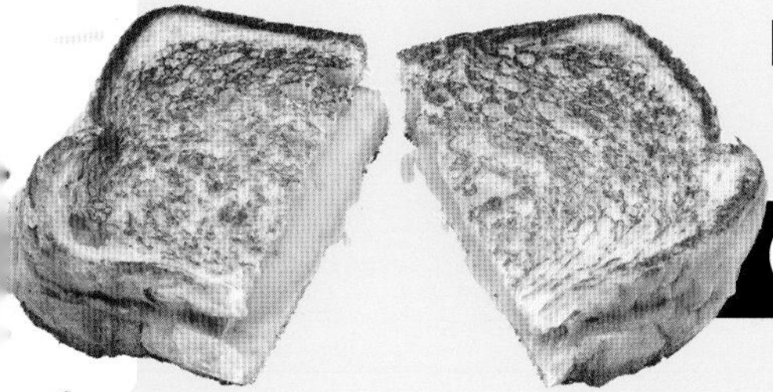

IN ROUND ROCK, TEXAS,
**HOT DOGS ARE
WRAPPED** IN A
**GRILLED CHEESE
SANDWICH.**

IN ERIE, PENNSYLVANIA,
**THEY'RE SERVED
ON A BED** OF
COTTON CANDY!

SOME CREATURES LOVE STINKY FEET!

Mosquitoes
are more attracted
to people with
smelly feet.

SOME
U.S. PRESIDENTS
HAD

UNUSUAL
TASTES ...

Sorry,
CAN'T
STAY for
dinner!

WILLIAM H. HARRISON ENJOYED **SQUIRREL STEW.**

RICHARD M. NIXON PUT **KETCHUP** ON HIS **COTTAGE CHEESE.**

LYNDON B. JOHNSON LIKED HIS **SALAD CHOPPED** SO FINE HE COULD EAT IT WITH A **SPOON.**

73

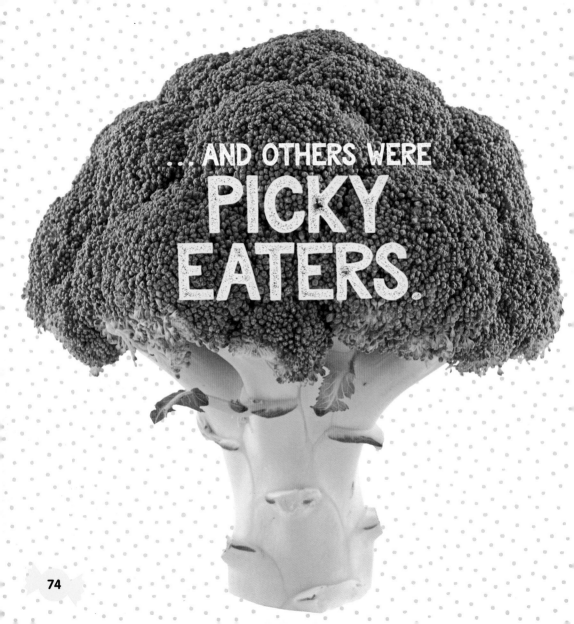

... AND OTHERS WERE
PICKY
EATERS.

BARACK OBAMA LOVES **SANDWICHES** BUT HATES **MAYONNAISE.**

GEORGE H. W. BUSH ONCE DECLARED THAT AS PRESIDENT OF THE UNITED STATES, HE DIDN'T HAVE TO EAT **BROCCOLI.**

HARRY TRUMAN REFUSED TO EAT ANY DISH WITH **ONIONS** IN IT.

First Lady Michelle Obama and local students in the White House Kitchen Garden

INSIDE THE
WHITE HOUSE
KITCHEN

The job of the U.S. president isn't easy—but there is one pretty nice perk: You get to live in the White House. There are 132 rooms, 35 bathrooms, 28 fireplaces, three elevators, and a kitchen with several chefs on hand to serve the first family's favorite meal or dinner for more than 100 guests. White House chefs are trained to prepare everything from hors d'oeuvres for the Queen of England to eggs for the annual White House Easter Egg Roll.

When President Barack Obama was in office, First Lady Michelle Obama planted the White House Kitchen Garden on the South Lawn. The 2,800-square-foot (260-sq-m) garden provided 2,000 pounds (907 kg) of food each year for the first family and White House guests. Any food not used was donated to local Washington, D.C., charities.

This wasn't the first time the White House had its own garden. John Adams, the second president, planted one in 1797. And during World War II, First Lady Eleanor Roosevelt planted a garden and encouraged all Americans to do the same in their own backyards to help ease wartime food shortages. Veggies for a victory!

Diana Hopkins tends the White House Victory Garden, 1943.

EGYPTIAN TOMBS

HELD MORE THAN JUST MUMMIES.

Pharaoh Khufu's Great Pyramid of Giza housed a **144-FOOT (44-m) SHIP.**

BOARD GAMES were included in tombs to help the dead pass the time in the afterlife.

King Tutankhamun had **SIX CHARIOTS** buried alongside him in his tomb.

Jars containing the **ORGANS** of mummified Egyptians were often buried with them for use in the afterlife.

Greetings.
I'm your
GREAT-
GRANDBOT!

ROBOTIC TOYS
HAVE BEEN AROUND FOR CENTURIES.

In the early **13TH CENTURY**, Arab inventor Ismail al-Jazari built a **FLOATING ORCHESTRA** of four **ROBOTIC MUSICIANS** that played music while being rowed by **MECHANICAL OARSMEN.**

A MECHANICAL DUCK created by French inventor Jacques de Vaucanson in **1739** **"ATE" GRAIN** and **"POOPED" PELLETS.**

In 1768, Swiss inventor **PIERRE JAQUET-DROZ** constructed a **MECHANICAL BOY** that moved its head, blinked its eyes, and **DIPPED A QUILL PEN** in ink to write up to **40 LETTERS** on paper.

HONEYBEES ARE

HARD
WORKERS.

Only 89 MORE to go!

HONEYBEES VISIT UP TO **100 FLOWERS** ON EVERY **BACK-AND-FORTH** TRIP TO THE HIVE.

THEY BEAT THEIR WINGS **200 TIMES A SECOND** AS THEY FLY FROM **FLOWER TO FLOWER** TO COLLECT POLLEN.

TO MAKE **ONE POUND (.45 KG) OF HONEY,** WORKER BEES FLY **55,000 MILES** **(88,500 KM)** AND VISIT **TWO MILLION** FLOWERS.

Every year, **millions of people** visit the weeklong **Sapporo Snow Festival** in Japan to view immense **snow sculptures** before they **melt.**

After the artwork **"Girl with Balloon"** was bought for **$1.4 million** at a 2018 auction, a device in the frame **shredded half the painting.**

An artist in Wisconsin, U.S.A., has made **edible sculptures** of celebrities, an aircraft carrier, deer, and football helmets out of **cheddar cheese.**

SOME AIRLINES TAKE IN-FLIGHT ENTERTAINMENT TO THE NEXT LEVEL.

A **U.S.-BASED AIRLINE** SURPRISES PASSENGERS WITH LIVE **POP-UP CONCERTS** BY COUNTRY MUSICIANS.

A **SOUTH KOREAN AIRLINE** OFFERS **MAGIC SHOWS** AND **FORTUNE-TELLERS** ONBOARD.

BATS ARE UNIQUE FLIERS.

Bats **DROP FROM A PERCH to take flight** rather than taking off from the ground.

Bat wings are made of **thin, flexible skin,** allowing the flying mammals to fold their wings and **CHANGE DIRECTION QUICKLY.**

Up, up, and AWAY!

Instead of feathers, **bat wings are covered in tiny hairs** used to DETECT SMALL CHANGES IN THE WIND.

SOME ANIMALS TAKE TO THE SKY BUT **DON'T ACTUALLY** FLY.

WALLACE'S FLYING FROGS HAVE MEMBRANES BETWEEN THEIR TOES THAT GIVE THEM LIFT WHEN **JUMPING BETWEEN TREES.**

Ready for **TAKE-OFF!**

PALM-SIZE SUGAR GLIDERS CAN **GLIDE** HALF THE LENGTH OF A SOCCER FIELD.

WHEN A **DRACO LIZARD** JUMPS, SKIN BETWEEN ITS RIBS OPENS LIKE AN UMBRELLA, HELPING IT **GLIDE.**

FLYING SNAKES FAN THEIR RIBS WHEN THEY **SAIL BETWEEN TREES,** WHICH IMPROVES THEIR AERODYNAMICS.

91

SURFING
CAN BE
EXTREME.

In 2017, Rodrigo Koxa rode an **80-FOOT (24-m)-TALL WAVE** off the coast of Nazaré, Portugal—the largest ever ridden.

"Surfers" ride sandboards down a **1,150-FOOT** (351-m)-**TALL DUNE** in Chile known as **DRAGÓN HILL,** which is taller than the **EIFFEL TOWER.**

Some surfers get **TOWED OUT BY JET SKIS** to reach monster waves.

Gary Saavedra surfed behind **A WAVE-MAKING BOAT** in the Panama Canal to ride one wave for more than **40 MILES** (64 km).

SOME ANIMALS
SLEEP
A LOT ...

On average, **DOMESTIC CATS** snooze for about two-thirds of a **24-HOUR DAY**.

Just getting **SOME BEAUTY REST!**

KOALAS sleep in eucalyptus trees for up to **18 HOURS A DAY.**

This body armor is a **TIRING** load to carry!

GIANT ARMADILLOS spend about **75 PERCENT OF EACH DAY** asleep.

... AND SOME

HARDLY SLEEP AT ALL.

NOTHING gets by me!

GIRAFFES enter a deep-sleep stage for only about 30 MINUTES A DAY.

OLDER HONEYBEES take "BEE-NAPS" for 15 to 30 SECONDS at a time, which adds up to ABOUT AN HOUR and a half of sleep a night.

The ALPINE SWIFT can fly for 200 DAYS straight by resting one half of its brain at a time.

Only ONE SIDE of a DOLPHIN'S BRAIN SLEEPS at a time.

Some gingerbread houses are MANSIONS.

THE **GRAND AMERICA HOTEL** IN SALT LAKE CITY, UTAH, U.S.A., HAD A TWO-STORY GINGERBREAD HOUSE HELD TOGETHER WITH 350 POUNDS (160 KG) OF RICE KRISPIES CEREAL TREATS.

YOU CAN **EAT INSIDE** A GINGERBREAD HOUSE IN AUSTIN, TEXAS, U.S.A.

A GINGERBREAD HOUSE IN ATLANTA, GEORGIA, U.S.A., DOUBLED AS A **CANDY SHOP.**

Some pirates went to EXTREMES TO STRIKE FEAR INTO PEOPLE.

When going into battle, **Blackbeard** lit fire to pieces of cord fastened **UNDER HIS HAT** so that the smoke twisted around his face.

Legend holds that **Anne Bonny** held an **AX OVER A MANNEQUIN TO TRICK—AND SCARE—SAILORS** on a French merchant ship passing by.

Ahoy, **MATEY!**

Postcard depicting pirates from the 1600s

IT'S A PIRATE'S LIFE

Pirates were a rowdy bunch. After all, they made a living by looting treasure and generally causing trouble. But what was life on a pirate ship really like? Lawlessness often reigned, but some aspects were surprisingly civilized.

By studying accounts that pirates left behind, historians can get a picture of life onboard. Before setting sail, all the pirates on a voyage would agree to a written code of behavior. Crews would elect a pirate captain, and each pirate's vote had equal weight. Pirates could remove their captain for a number of reasons, from being too timid to making bad decisions.

Captains didn't get special treatment, either. They ate the same food and slept in the same conditions. Crews also voted on whether to attack a ship or leave it alone. And booty, for the most part, was evenly shared. Pirates even had a form of insurance. If a pirate was injured on the job, he or she would be compensated. And if worthy of a reward for a job well done, they could receive a bonus.

But while life onboard may have been democratic, it wasn't always a sure thing—you could be forced overboard.

A battle between two ships, *Kent* and *Confiance*

SOME ANIMALS CAN LIVE UNDER EXTREME CONDITIONS.

TARDIGRADES, also called water bears, are only .04 inch (1 mm) and can withstand temperatures from **MINUS 328°F** (-200°C) **TO 304°F** (151°C).

BRINE SHRIMP live in water **10 TIMES SALTIER** than the ocean.

METHANE ICE WORMS are **BURIED IN MOUNDS OF FROZEN GAS** on the ocean floor in the Gulf of Mexico and feast on bacteria.

FLOWERS CAN TELL TIME.

Guess I don't need this ANYMORE!

MOON-FLOWERS bloom only at **night**.

The flowers of the **FOUR-O'CLOCK PLANT** open in **late afternoon** and **close by morning**.

The **SUNFLOWER** moves its head from **east to west** throughout the day, **following the sun**.

107

ASTRONAUTS
HAVE LEFT A LOT OF THINGS ON
THE **MOON.**

Astronauts have left **SEVERAL BAGS OF URINE** on the moon.

Eugene Cernan, the last American astronaut to visit the moon, in 1972, **CARVED HIS DAUGHTER'S INITIALS** into the moon's surface.

Where did I put my KEYS?

Jettison bag

Buzz Aldrin and Neil Armstrong **TOSSED THEIR BOOTS** from the hatch of their spacecraft before returning to Earth.

SIX AMERICAN FLAGS have been placed on the moon—now they are all bleached white from the sun.

Alan Shepard hit a **GOLF BALL** on the moon that traveled for miles.

BACON
ISN'T JUST FOR
BREAKFAST.

PERFUME THE AIR WITH **A BACON-SCENTED AIR FRESHENER.**

Say WHAT?!

BITE INTO **CHOCOLATE-COVERED BACON** FOR A SWEET-AND-SAVORY TREAT.

PUT A **BACON BANDAGE** ON A SMALL SCRATCH.

CRUNCH ON **BACON-AND-CHEESE-FLAVORED CRICKETS.**

CRICK-ETTES

Bacon & Cheese
Net Wt. 1g

BICYCLES HAVE
A LONG HISTORY.

Where's my HELMET?

An illustration of
Curiosity rover
on Mars

A BICYCLE MANUFACTURER BUILT THE **FRAME FOR NASA'S CURIOSITY ROVER,** WHICH IS LOOKING FOR SIGNS OF **LIFE ON MARS.**

THE **GIANT FRONT WHEEL** OF THE **PENNY-FARTHING,** A BICYCLE POPULAR IN THE 1870S, WAS **TALLER THAN A 10-YEAR-OLD KID.**

IN 1955, A BICYCLE COMPANY INTRODUCED A BIKE WITH **A RADIO MOUNTED ON THE CROSSBAR.**

IN 1817, KARL VON DRAIS INVENTED AN EARLY VERSION OF A TWO-WHEELED BICYCLE—BUT **IT DIDN'T HAVE PEDALS OR BRAKES.**

FIERCE-LOOKING MARINE IGUANAS
OF THE GALÁPAGOS ISLANDS
ARE ACTUALLY
GENTLE LIZARDS.

Their signature sound is **achoo!** They **sneeze often to get rid of salt** from the seawater they drink.

Marine iguanas have **razor-sharp teeth,** but they don't use them to attack prey—the teeth **scrape algae off rocks underwater.**

White "hats" sometimes form on their head from the **buildup of the salt they sneeze out.**

Galápagos tortoise

THE WEIRDLY WILD ANIMALS OF THE GALÁPAGOS

The Galápagos Islands host unique and unusual animals.
Separated from mainland South America by 600 miles (965 km) of water, the species that live there have evolved by adapting to the conditions on each of the islands. That means there are species on the Galápagos not found anywhere else.

Galápagos tortoises, which can grow to be four feet (1.2 m) long and 475 pounds (216 kg), have lived on the islands for three million years. Today, they are vulnerable to extinction due to threats from non-native species (like rats that eat their eggs) and climate change.

The flightless cormorant, which lives on two of the Galápagos Islands, found its perfect niche. It has adapted to dive for its food and can no longer fly. The cormorant's wings are about a third of the size of what it would need for flight, but it uses its powerful legs and webbed toes to dive underwater for octopus and eel.

The two species of frigate birds have names that say much about them: the great frigate bird and the magnificent frigate bird. The males of both species attract females by inflating a thin, bright red sac on their throat with air. Talk about showing off!

Frigate bird

ASTEROIDS MAY BE
CLOSER
THAN YOU THINK.

IN FEBRUARY 2013, AN ASTEROID ENTERED EARTH'S ATMOSPHERE NEAR CHELYABINSK, RUSSIA, **CREATING A METEOR BRIGHTER THAN THE SUN.**

That's close in **SPACE SPEAK!**

ON HALLOWEEN 2019, A SMALL ASTEROID PASSED WITHIN **3,850 MILES** (6,200 KM) **OF EARTH.**

YOU CAN TOUCH A REMNANT OF A SMALL ASTEROID, KNOWN AS **THE CAPE YORK METEORITE,** IN THE AMERICAN MUSEUM OF NATURAL HISTORY IN NEW YORK CITY.

Easy PEASY.

SOME ANIMALS ARE SUPER

ATHLETES.

OWNERS CAN **TEST THEIR DOGS' SPEED** AND AGILITY BY TRAINING THEM TO **RACE THROUGH TUNNELS, JUMP THROUGH TIRES,** AND **WEAVE THROUGH POLES.**

A RABBIT IN FINLAND CAN PERFORM **20 TRICKS** IN **JUST ONE MINUTE,** INCLUDING A **"PAW" FIVE.**

CASPA, A LLAMA IN WALES, CAN JUMP OVER A NEARLY **FOUR-FOOT (1.2-M) HURDLE.**

SOME FROGS CAN **JUMP** MORE THAN **18 FEET (5.5 M)—LONGER** THAN A MINIVAN!

BRIDGES CAN BE MADE OF MANY THINGS.

THE ANCIENT INCA OF SOUTH AMERICA made hundreds of bridges out of woven grasses, including a **120-foot** (37-m)-long span that still stretches over the **APURÍMAC RIVER IN PERU.**

A SUSPENSION BRIDGE in Meghalaya, India, is made out of **tree roots.**

More than **55 tons** (50 t) of **RECYCLED PLASTIC** went into a **90-foot** (27-m)-long bridge over the **RIVER TWEED IN SCOTLAND.**

123

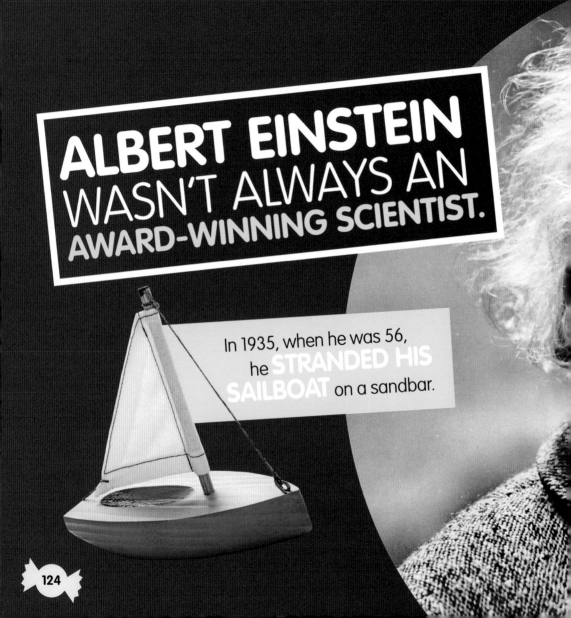

ALBERT EINSTEIN WASN'T ALWAYS AN AWARD-WINNING SCIENTIST.

In 1935, when he was 56, he **STRANDED HIS SAILBOAT** on a sandbar.

AS A CHILD, one of his headmasters said he would never **AMOUNT TO MUCH.**

He **FAILED** his **FIRST ENTRANCE** exam to get into college, and, once accepted, he often **SKIPPED CLASS.**

SOMETIMES
SOMETHING
GOOD
COMES FROM A
MISTAKE.

A SCIENTIST TRYING TO INVENT A STRONG ADHESIVE ACCIDENTALLY **INVENTED A WEAK ONE THAT COULD BE USED OVER AND OVER,** WHICH LED TO THE CREATION OF **POST-IT NOTES.**

POPSICLES WERE INVENTED AFTER AN 11-YEAR-OLD BOY **LEFT A SUGARY DRINK WITH A STICK IN IT** ON HIS PORCH, WHERE IT **FROZE OVERNIGHT.**

HOPING TO CREATE A SUBSTITUTE FOR BREAD, BROTHERS WILLIAM AND JOHN KELLOGG ACCIDENTALLY INVENTED **CORNFLAKES.**

MANTIS SHRIMP AREN'T SHRIMPY.

THEY **PUNCH THEIR PREY** WITH **HINGED ARMS** THAT HAVE HEAVY CLUBS AT THE END.

WITH **EACH PUNCH,** A CLUB'S EDGE TRAVELS AT ABOUT **50 MILES AN HOUR** (80 KM/H).

THEY CAN **"THROW" A PUNCH** FASTER THAN THE **BLINK** OF AN EYE.

I'm a paw-some CHOICE!

PETS CAN **WIN** U.S. **ELECTIONS**, TOO.

STUBBS THE CAT WAS **HONORARY MAYOR** OF AN ALASKAN TOWN.

BRYNNETH PAWLTRO, A PIT BULL, WAS **ELECTED MAYOR** OF A SMALL KENTUCKY TOWN.

THREE DIFFERENT GOATS HAVE BEEN THE **MAYOR** OF LAJITAS, TEXAS.

BOSCO THE LABRADOR RETRIEVER BEAT TWO PEOPLE TO BECOME **HONORARY MAYOR** OF A CALIFORNIA TOWN FOR 13 YEARS.

THE *TITANIC* WAS GIGANTIC.

The combined weight of the ship's **three anchors** was more than that of **four African elephants.**

At **882 feet** (270 m), the *Titanic* was longer than **two football fields**, making it the **largest human-made** moving object on Earth in 1912.

The ship had **four** smokestacks, each taller than **three stacked giraffes.**

NIC

SOME **ANIMALS** ARE **QUITE HANDY.**

Packing it in after a busy day ...

Some octopuses **LUG TWO HALVES** of a **COCONUT SHELL** to use as a hiding place—they crawl inside and close up the two halves.

Chimpanzees create **"SPONGES"** out of leaves and use sticks to "fish" termites out of their nests.

To reach food, New Caledonian crows **USE STICKS** they have shaped into tools.

A SNOW LEOPARD CAN WITHSTAND THE COLD.

It wraps its **fluffy three-foot (0.9-m)-long tail** around its body for **warmth.**

The snow leopard's **wide nose** **warms air** **before** it enters its **lungs.**

Snow leopard mothers **use the** **fur they've shed** to **line their den.**

Its **tail can** **store fat** in case it doesn't get enough food in winter.

Did you hear the NEWZZZZ?

THERE'S A **BIG BUZZ** ABOUT **CICADAS.**

UP CLOSE, THE NOISE CAN **BE LOUDER** THAN **A DIESEL TRAIN.**

EACH OF THE **3,000 DIFFERENT SPECIES** OF CICADA HAS A **DIFFERENT "BUZZ."**

THE LOUD HUM OF SOME CICADAS CAN BE HEARD FROM **A MILE (1.6 KM)** AWAY.

TO MAKE THEIR **LOUD BUZZING,** MALE **CICADAS VIBRATE** A MEMBRANE CALLED **A TYMBAL** ON THEIR **TORSO.**

Next stop ... BROADWAY!

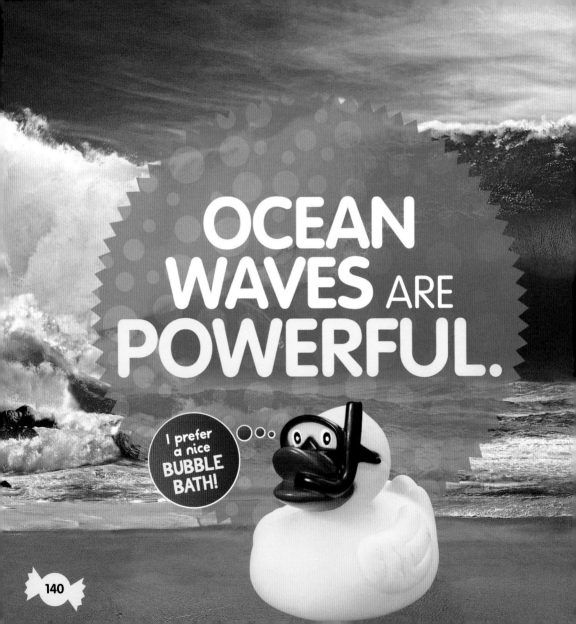

Tsunamis can travel as fast as a **jet airplane** in **deep ocean water.**

Tidal waves in the Bay of Fundy off the coast of **Nova Scotia, Canada,** can create **12-foot** (3.7-m)-**tall rapids.**

Giant rogue waves, which can be as tall as a **10-story building,** have caused **supertankers to sink.**

HARNESSING THE ENERGY OF
OCEAN WAVES

Surf's up! The ocean is a great place to relax, but it's also full of energy. Researchers are working on devices that use wave power to create electricity. Waves provide a clean alternative to power made from burning fossil fuels. And since water is about 800 times denser than air, waves carry more energy than wind. Some scientists think that by 2050, wave energy could provide 10 percent of the world's electricity.

Harnessing wave power isn't a new idea. Engineers have been working on it for more than a hundred years. In the early 1900s, a few inventors in California, U.S.A., experimented with "wave motors." One contraption on the Huntington Beach Wharf in 1909 powered lights along the pier, but ultimately, the device was swept out to sea.

But scientists kept experimenting. Today's devices are similar to floats that "ride" the swells of waves. Some are like long moving snakes, while others are buoys that bob up and down. In 2016, off the coast of Oahu, Hawaii, U.S.A., a 45-ton (41-t) device harnessed wave motion to make electricity that traveled to the shore through an underwater cable.

Waves have another benefit, too. They keep coming, all day and all night—the perfect renewable resource!

Wave energy buoy near Oahu, Hawaii, U.S.A.

A MILE CAN BE REALLY

SHORT ...

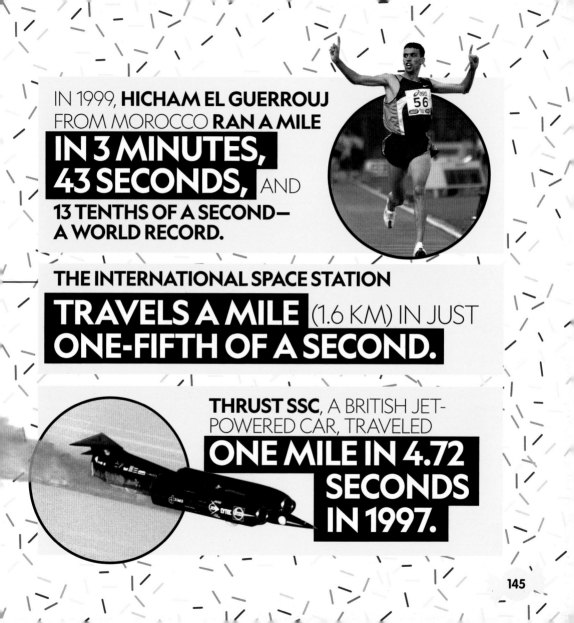

IN 1999, **HICHAM EL GUERROUJ** FROM MOROCCO **RAN A MILE**

IN 3 MINUTES, 43 SECONDS, AND

13 TENTHS OF A SECOND— A WORLD RECORD.

THE INTERNATIONAL SPACE STATION

TRAVELS A MILE (1.6 KM) IN JUST **ONE-FIFTH OF A SECOND.**

THRUST SSC, A BRITISH JET-POWERED CAR, TRAVELED

ONE MILE IN 4.72 SECONDS IN 1997.

...OR REALLY

LONG.

ABOUT **126,500** **CARPENTER ANTS** WOULD HAVE TO LINE UP TO **STRETCH A MILE.**

IT WOULD TAKE **825,305 NICKELS** STACKED ON TOP OF ONE ANOTHER TO MAKE **A MILE-HIGH COLUMN.**

Get ready, get set ...

A SLOTH, MOVING AT ITS **NORMAL DAILY PACE,** WOULD NEED **43 DAYS TO TRAVEL** A MILE.

TRASH CAN BE GREEN.

LANDFILLS CAN CREATE ENERGY BY BURNING THE **METHANE GAS** THAT **DECOMPOSING TRASH PRODUCES.**

PEOPLE WALK ON NEARLY **TWO MILES** (3.2 KM) OF TRAILS BY MOUNT TRASHMORE, **A SIX-STORY-TALL MOUND** IN A PARK MADE FROM **COMPACTED TRASH** IN VIRGINIA BEACH, VIRGINIA, U.S.A.

IN SWEDEN, MORE THAN **30 POWER PLANTS** BURN TRASH **TO HEAT HOUSES.**

Man, I was gonna paw right through that bag!

149

ELEPHANTS HAVE THICK SKIN.

An **elephant's skin** is **50 times thicker** than yours.

Their skin can weigh as much as **2,000 pounds** (900 kg).

2000.00 LB

Cracks in their **skin** can hold **water** to **cool them**—more than **10 times** that of a **smooth surface.**

ANIMALS HAVE
MIND-BLOWING
WAYS
OF SURVIVING
THE WINTER.

To hibernate, **marmots** reduce their body temperature by **50°F** (28°C) and **slow their breathing.**

Some turtles stay in water **under pond ice** and take in **oxygen through their rear end.**

The temperature inside **male emperor penguins'** huddles can reach nearly **100°F** (38°C) in the bitter Antarctic cold.

A wood frog's heart stops beating and **special proteins freeze** its blood.

THERE IS A LOT OF WATER IN THE SKY.

Large "rivers" of water vapor in the sky can hold as much as 15 times the amount of water that flows out of the Mississippi River.

That one was a SOAKER!

All the water droplets in some big clouds weigh about as much as a **747 airplane.**

You can **mail** **postcards** from **weird** **places.**

Does anyone have an EXTRA STAMP?

MAIL

DAILY
7:32 AM
10:00 AM
12:30 PM
3:15 PM
6:05 PM

SUNDAY
9:30 AM

4:55 PM

156

You can DIVE 10 FEET (3 m) below the water's surface to reach an UNDERWATER POST OFFICE off the island nation of VANUATU.

A colony of 3,000 GENTOO PENGUINS in Port Lockroy, Antarctica, SHARES THEIR BREEDING GROUNDS with a POST OFFICE.

At Post Office Bay in the GALÁPAGOS ISLANDS, there is a WOODEN BARREL where tourists pick up dropped-off letters and deliver them to the mainland for FREE.

BUILDINGS CAN BE GREEN.

In Dubai, United Arab Emirates, the **SUSTAINABLE CITY** development uses solar power to produce **ALL ITS ENERGY.**

There are about **1.7 MILLION NATIVE PLANTS** growing on the roof of the **CALIFORNIA ACADEMY OF SCIENCES** in San Francisco, California, U.S.A.

THE SHANGHAI TOWER in China, the second tallest building in the world, has a **CLEAR SECOND SKIN** that helps insulate it to **SAVE ENERGY.**

159

GOLF HAS SOME WILD TERMINOLOGY.

This course is HOGGING my ground!

A "Texas wedge" means using a **putter** to **hit a ball** that's way off the green.

A ball **"in the drink"** is a ball hit into **the water.**

A "stinger" is a ball **hit low in the air** so that it travels **under the wind.**

A "chicken stick" is a club used **off the tee** that's meant to help a golfer **hit accurately** but **not very far.**

Some sports teams have UNUSUAL MASCOTS.

THE UNIVERSITY OF CALIFORNIA, SANTA CRUZ, IS HOME TO THE **BANANA SLUGS**.

THE **BOLL WEEVIL**—A BEETLE PEST TO COTTON GROWERS—IS THE MASCOT OF THE UNIVERSITY OF ARKANSAS AT MONTICELLO.

THE COLORADO ROCKIES BASEBALL TEAM CHOSE A DINOSAUR AS THEIR MASCOT AFTER WORKERS FOUND A **TRICERATOPS** SKULL DURING CONSTRUCTION OF THE TEAM'S STADIUM.

163

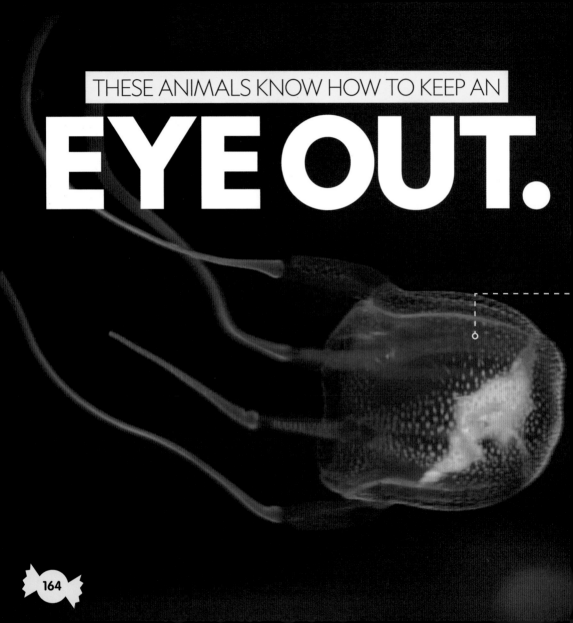

THESE ANIMALS KNOW HOW TO KEEP AN

EYE OUT.

GOATS'
RECTANGULAR-SHAPED EYES
LOOK OUT FOR PREDATORS WHILE THEY GRAZE WITH THEIR **HEAD DOWN.**

BOX JELLYFISH HAVE **24 EYES!**

CHAMELEONS CAN **MOVE EACH EYE INDEPENDENTLY,** ALLOWING THEM TO **LOOK IN TWO DIFFERENT DIRECTIONS** WITH A **360-DEGREE VIEW.**

TERMITES ARE
INSECT
ENGINEERS.

Colonies of termites in southern Africa build **mounds nearly 30 feet** (9 m) **tall.**

Termites race to repair any break in the mound.

They **create tunnels** within the mound walls to **keep the air inside** at a comfortable temperature.

CALIFORNIA COAST REDWOODS ARE THE **WORLD'S TALLEST TREES.**

CHANDELIER
TREE

Did I mention I'm afraid of **HEIGHTS?**

It would take a **STACK OF MORE** than **20 GIRAFFES** to **REACH THE TOP** of the **TALLEST REDWOOD.**

You can **DRIVE A CAR THROUGH THE TRUNK** of a coast redwood along the **"AVENUE OF THE GIANTS," A 31-MILE** (50-km)-long scenic drive in Northern California, U.S.A.

Scientists who **CLIMB TO THE TOP OF THE TREES** must use **HANDHELD RADIOS** to communicate with **PEOPLE ON THE GROUND.**

ANIMALS LIKE TO
SING.

The superb lyrebird from southern Australia **mimics sounds from its environment**—including **HUMAN-MADE SOUNDS**, such as **hammering** and a **camera shutter clicking**—in its songs.

Male humpback whales **"sing" songs** that are a series of **GROANS, WHOOPS, WHISTLES,** and **BARKS,** which are thought to **attract mates.**

CLOUDS CREATE
BEAUTIFUL ART.

FILMY SHEETS OF RARE **NACREOUS CLOUDS** SHINE IN **IRIDESCENT COLORS.**

LENTICULAR CLOUDS OVER **A MOUNTAIN** CAN LOOK LIKE **A STACK OF PANCAKES.**

IN THE TROPICS, CLOUDS CAN **STRETCH UPWARD** FOR **12 MILES** (19 KM) BEFORE FORMING **A FLAT, ANVIL-SHAPED TOP.**

CIRRUS CLOUDS, FOUND HIGH IN THE ATMOSPHERE, LOOK LIKE **WISPY, DELICATE STRANDS OF HAIR.**

Arctic animals can EAT MORE than you can.

Hold the **KETCHUP**, please.

WALRUSES can devour up to **60 CLAMS** during one dive to the seafloor.

ARCTIC WOLVES can eat up to **22 POUNDS** (10 kg) **OF MEAT** at a time— that's as much as **88 HAMBURGERS!**

A **POLAR BEAR'S** stomach can hold more than **150 POUNDS** (68 kg) **OF FOOD**— equal to **2,560 HOT DOGS.**

175

ANIMALS CAN BE EXPERT NAVIGATORS.

Some **MONARCH BUTTERFLIES,** the only butterfly known to migrate, journey about **3,000 MILES** (4,800 km) from eastern North America to the Sierra Madre mountains in Mexico.

ARCTIC TERNS travel from breeding grounds in the Arctic to spend summers in Antarctica—an annual migration of approximately **25,000 MILES** (40,200 km).

LEATHERBACK SEA TURTLES travel from feeding areas back to **TROPICAL BEACHES** where **THEY WERE BORN.**

Sandhill cranes

AMAZING ANIMAL
MIGRATIONS

Some animals trek hundreds—or even thousands—of miles on long-distance migrations. Migrating birds take to the skies while sharks and whales swim across oceans. Even rattlesnakes and red crabs journey to the same area year after year to have their young. These journeys are not only incredible feats of endurance, but also of instinct. Somehow, these animals just know how to reach their destinations.

Take sandhill cranes. Flocks move north to have their young, with some flying from southwestern Texas, U.S.A., across the Bering Strait to breeding grounds in Siberia—a trip of some 5,000 miles (8,000 km). During their trip, more than 80 percent of the world's sandhill cranes stop at the same place to rest and eat—the Platte River in central Nebraska, U.S.A.

Scientists are working to unravel some migration mysteries. They put colorful bands on the legs of sandhill cranes so that bird-watchers can report sightings and keep track of movements. Small tracking devices communicate information about location, which researchers use to plot pathways. Whether it's Earth's magnetic field, navigation by sense of smell or sight, or an understanding of celestial patterns, these animals on the move are mesmerizing.

One step at a time...

THE INTERNET
WASN'T ALWAYS JUST A
CLICK
AWAY.

In the 1980s, **ONLY GOVERNMENT RESEARCHERS** had **INTERNET ACCESS,** but today more than five out of every 10 people in the world can go online.

In 1993, it took **MORE THAN 24 HOURS** to download a movie onto a computer using a dial-up internet connection.

If only I could type and look up **TREATS** and **TOYS.**

In 1995, reporters attended a seminar in Europe to learn **HOW TO "SURF" THE WEB.**

181

BACTERIA DON'T JUST

MAKE YOU SICK.

SCIENTISTS HAVE USED A KIND OF BACTERIA FOUND IN HUMAN INTESTINES TO MAKE A **RENEWABLE FUEL.**

Did somebody say **CHEESE?**

BACTERIA ARE USED TO MAKE **CHEESE, SAUERKRAUT, AND YOGURT.**

THEY CAN **DETECT POLLUTION** IN **LAKES AND RIVERS.**

THEY CAN **CONTROL PESTS IN PLANTS.**

People add **WHITE CHALK** to a **GIGANTIC FIGURE OF A HORSE** that was cut into a hill about **3,000 YEARS** ago in Oxfordshire, England, to help preserve it.

ASTRONAUTS on the International Space Station took a photograph of **RAIKOKE VOLCANO** on the Kuril Islands as it **ERUPTED IN 2019.**

WOODLAND INDIANS created a **214-FOOT** (65-m)-tall **EARTHEN MOUND** in the form of a man about **1,000 YEARS** ago in what is today central Wisconsin, U.S.A.

...WHILE OTHERS REVEAL MORE WHEN SEEN FROM THE INSIDE.

Doughnuts? I'm getting HUNGRY.

Under a **MICROSCOPE**, red blood cells look like **DOUGHNUTS**, but with squishy middles instead of holes, a shape that lets them **SQUEEZE** through small blood vessels.

Researchers have invented **A BODY SCANNER** that can capture **3D IMAGES** of the inside of a human body in just **ONE SECOND.**

HURRICANE HUNTERS fly inside the calm **12- TO 30-MILE** (20- to 50-km)-wide eye of a hurricane to **LEARN ABOUT THE STORM.**

LAKES CAN BE

SURPRISING.

THE DEAD SEA, A LAKE ON THE BORDER BETWEEN ISRAEL AND JORDAN, IS ALMOST **10 TIMES SALTIER** THAN THE OCEAN.

BACTERIA IN **LAKE HILLIER** ON MIDDLE ISLAND OFF THE SOUTHWEST COAST OF AUSTRALIA COLORS ITS **WATER PINK.**

ABOUT **7,700 YEARS AGO, THE DEEPEST LAKE** IN THE UNITED STATES, **CRATER LAKE** IN OREGON, WAS A VOLCANO.

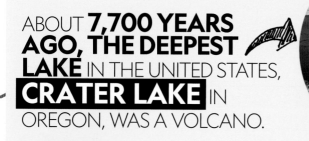

THE GREAT LAKES IN NORTH AMERICA HOLD MORE THAN **20 PERCENT** OF THE WORLD'S **SURFACE FRESHWATER.**

Robert to the RESCUE!

190

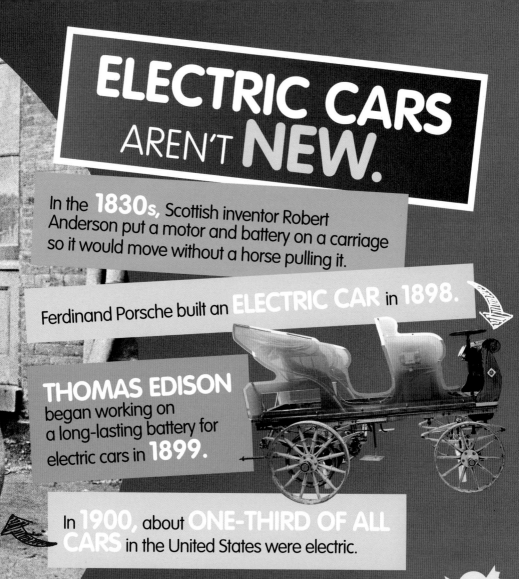

ELECTRIC CARS AREN'T NEW.

In the **1830s**, Scottish inventor Robert Anderson put a motor and battery on a carriage so it would move without a horse pulling it.

Ferdinand Porsche built an **ELECTRIC CAR** in **1898.**

THOMAS EDISON began working on a long-lasting battery for electric cars in **1899.**

In **1900**, about **ONE-THIRD OF ALL CARS** in the United States were electric.

That is ONE LUCKY DOG.

AMERICAN PRESIDENTS LOVED THEIR PETS ...

Legend has it that George Washington laughed when he found out his French hound Vulcan had **run away** with a **ham** being prepared for a dinner at Mount Vernon.

First Lady Grace Coolidge took the family's **pet raccoon, Rebecca,** to White House Easter Egg Rolls **on a leash.**

I can still smell the **GINGER- BREAD** ...

George W. Bush's pet **Scottish terriers, Barney** and **Miss Beazley, starred in holiday videos** filmed around the White House.

... BUT SO DID **OTHER WORLD LEADERS.**

Don't I get a VOTE?

Stephen Harper, a former prime minister of Canada, held a **Facebook poll** to name his gray tabby cat.

In the early 19th century, Pope Leo XII carried around his pet **cat, Micetto, in his robe.**

Queen Elizabeth II of the United Kingdom took her **Pembroke Welsh corgi, Susan,** on her honeymoon.

In the 1940s, British prime minister **Winston Churchill's poodle, Rufus, slept** with him and **ate** at the family dinner table.

SOME ISLANDS CAN HIDE SECRETS.

IT IS **ILLEGAL** TO VISIT **NORTH SENTINEL ISLAND** IN THE INDIAN OCEAN AND **DISTURB THE INDIGENOUS PEOPLE** WHO LIVE THERE.

PALMYRA ATOLL, AN ISLAND IN THE MIDDLE OF THE **PACIFIC OCEAN,** IS RUMORED TO BE **HAUNTED** BY THE **GHOSTS** OF SHIPWRECKED SAILORS.

A LEGEND HOLDS THAT **CAPTAIN KIDD BURIED TREASURE** ON CHARLES ISLAND, CONNECTICUT, U.S.A.

See ya later, KIDS!

THE **END** CAN BE **UNUSUAL.**

BEFORE THE **ERA OF 24-HOUR TV,** SOME STATIONS IN THE UNITED STATES **ENDED THEIR BROADCASTS** WITH A **PATRIOTIC SONG** AND THEN **STATIC UNTIL MORNING.**

THE **LAST WORD** IN THE *OXFORD ENGLISH DICTIONARY* IS **ZYZZYVA,** A TYPE OF **SOUTH AMERICAN WEEVIL.**

THE WINNER OF THE **INDIANAPOLIS 500** DRINKS **A GLASS OF MILK** AT THE END OF THE **500-MILE** (805-KM) RACE TO CELEBRATE.

INDEX

INDEX

INDEX

Since 1888, the National Geographic Society has funded more than 14,000 research, conservation, education, and storytelling projects around the world. National Geographic Partners distributes a portion of the funds it receives from your purchase to National Geographic Society to support programs including the conservation of animals and their habitats. To learn more, visit natgeo.com/info.

For more information, visit nationalgeographic.com, call 1-877-873-6846, or write to the following address:

National Geographic Partners, LLC
1145 17th Street N.W.
Washington, D.C. 20036-4688 U.S.A.

For librarians and teachers: nationalgeographic.com/books/librarians-and-educators

More for kids from National Geographic: natgeokids.com

National Geographic Kids magazine inspires children to explore their world with fun yet educational articles on animals, science, nature, and more. Using fresh storytelling and amazing photography, *Nat Geo Kids* shows kids ages 6 to 14 the fascinating truth about the world—and why they should care.
kids.nationalgeographic.com/subscribe

For rights or permissions inquiries, please contact National Geographic Books Subsidiary Rights: bookrights@natgeo.com

Designed by Amanda Larsen and Julide Dengel

The publisher would like to thank Julie Beer, author and researcher; Michelle Harris, author and researcher; Grace Hill Smith, project manager; Avery Naughton and Paige Towler, project editors; Hilary Andrews and Sarah J. Mock, photo editors; Molly Reid, production editor; and Anne LeongSon and Gus Tello, production assistants.

Trade paperback ISBN: 978-1-4263-7250-6
Reinforced library binding ISBN: 978-1-4263-7251-3

Printed in China
21/PPS/1

That was YUMMY!